BUILDING

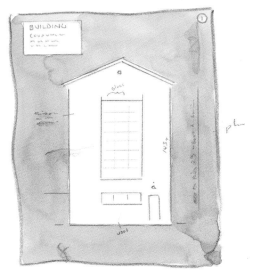

ELISHA COOPER

Greenwillow Books   New York

This is a deserted lot. It sits between two buildings

not far from downtown. It's mostly dirt, with a few

tufts of grass, some weeds, and two trees with

peeling bark. It's covered with broken glass and

trash. A chain-link fence keeps people out.

broken glass

One day an architect pulls up in a truck, bends back the fence,

leave, they take down the fence.

When they take down the fence. stakes into the ground. lay out string, and knock

and walks onto the lot. She unrolls blueprints and make notes on

them. She returns the next day with two workers

who set up

surveying tools,

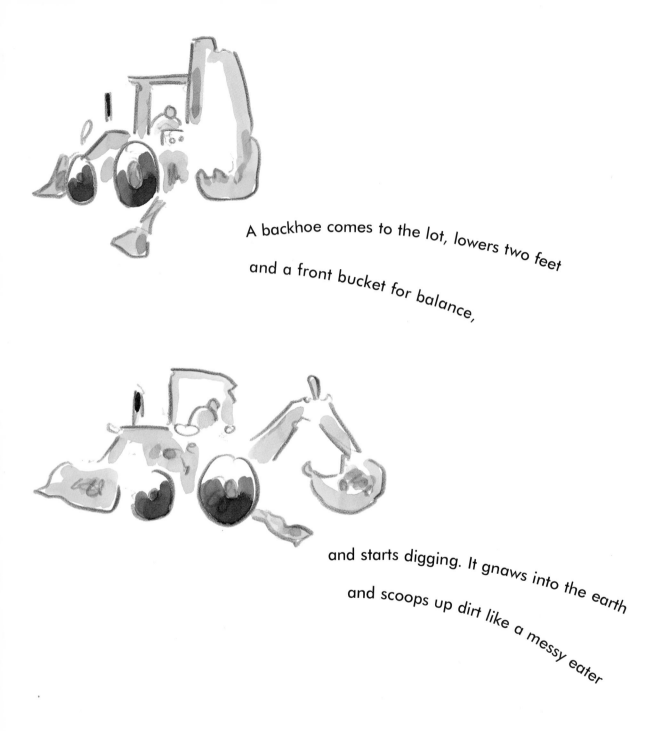

A backhoe comes to the lot, lowers two feet

and a front bucket for balance,

and starts digging. It gnaws into the earth

and scoops up dirt like a messy eater

trying to bring food to its mouth.

Then it hits something solid and stops.

A larger backhoe arrives, making deep ruts

in the ground, and pulls up a rock.

Trucks leave with dirt. Other trucks deliver materials: bricks, tools, nails, cement, shingles, ladders, stacks of wood banded with wire

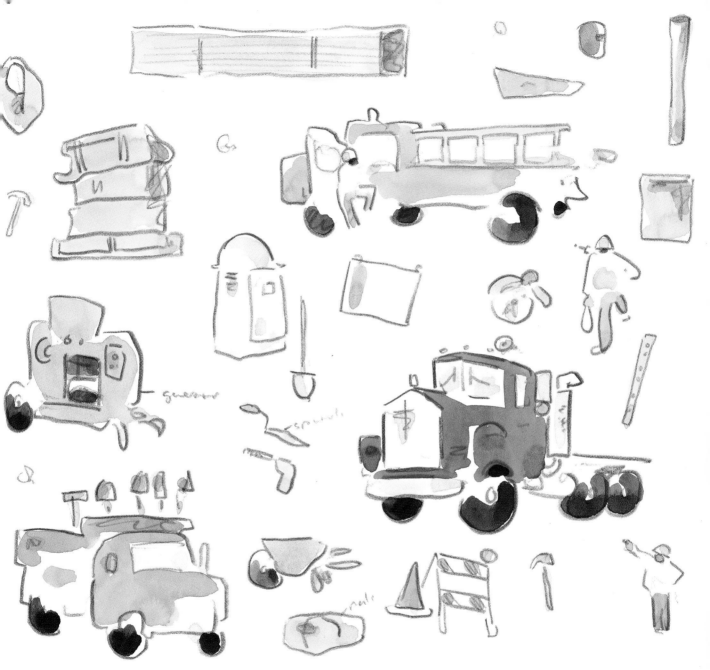

and painted red on the ends. Workers unload the trucks, which
beep when they roll backward: "Hey . . . you . . . watch . . . out."

A truck with a churning body pours concrete into wooden frames in the hole in the ground. The wooden frames mold and hold the concrete as it hardens. Inside the frames are steel rods that reinforce the foundation. The concrete smells like chalk.

A worker spreads and shovels the concrete. When her shovel hits a stone, it makes a sound that makes her shudder.

Another worker smoothes the wet concrete. His hands are crusted in gunk and he has to use his wrist to push his glasses up his nose.

One worker in overalls fills a wheelbarrow with a serving of lumpy mortar. It looks like a big tub of oatmeal.

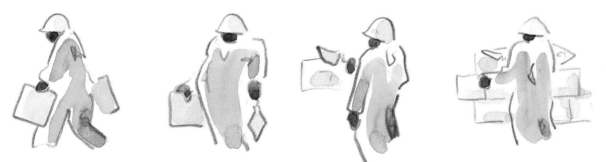

Workers gently toss blocks to each other, then stick them together using trowels lathered with mortar. A wall rises.

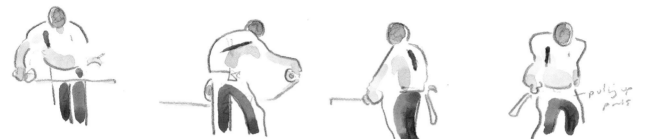

The foreman has so many tools on his belt his pants sag. A hammer wags from his belt like a tail. He measures boards and marks them with a rectangular blue pencil,

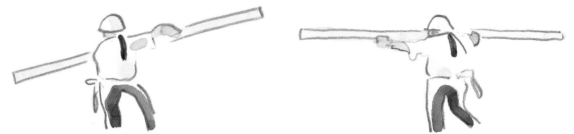

while another worker opens sawhorses, puts in ear plugs, and cuts boards for

the first floor. Hot sawdust fills the air and changes everyone's skin color.

As the building rises, workers add to the scaffolding. They hook

metal poles together and slide wooden planks on top of them.

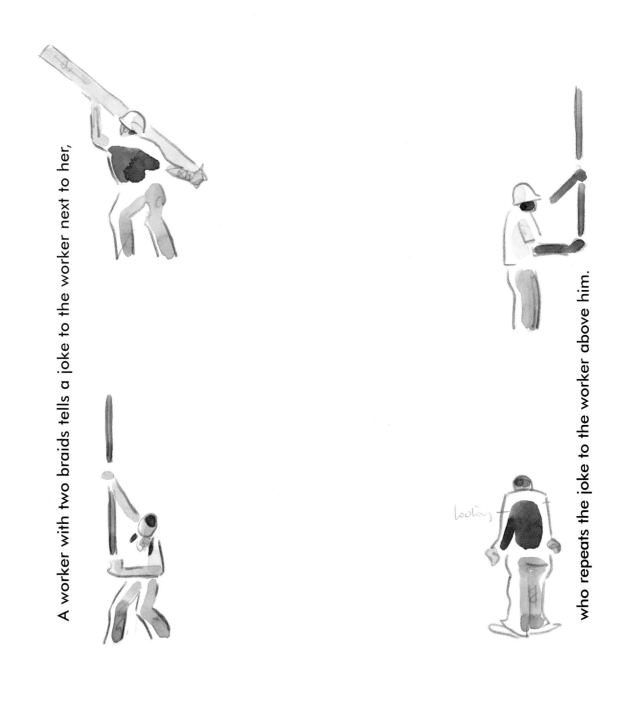

A worker with two braids tells a joke to the worker next to her,

who repeats the joke to the worker above him.

Every day at noon the lunch truck pulls up. Tool belts wait on rafters while

workers wait in line for bean burritos. Some workers walk down the block

and return with cartons of fried chicken. Others eat chocolate

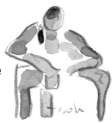

pudding  with plastic spoons. All slump against hard hats, lean

into each other, and talk—about their families, the union, last night's

game. One worker naps, one calls home. Another finds the Porta Potti.

Hammering echoes through the frame of the building. As nails are driven deeper into wood,

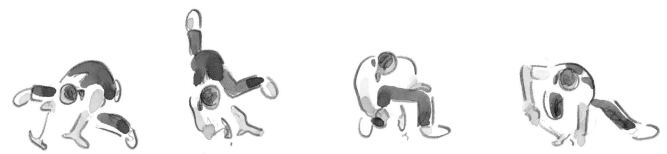

the sound rises higher in scale: "Do re me fa so la ti do." If a nail has to be pulled out with the

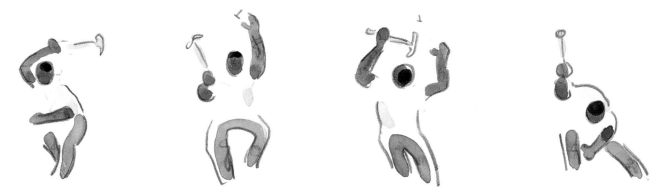

claw of the hammer, it screeches as if it were happy right where it was. One worker, with hands and arms so big they could juggle trucks, hits his nail into the wood with one stroke: "Do."

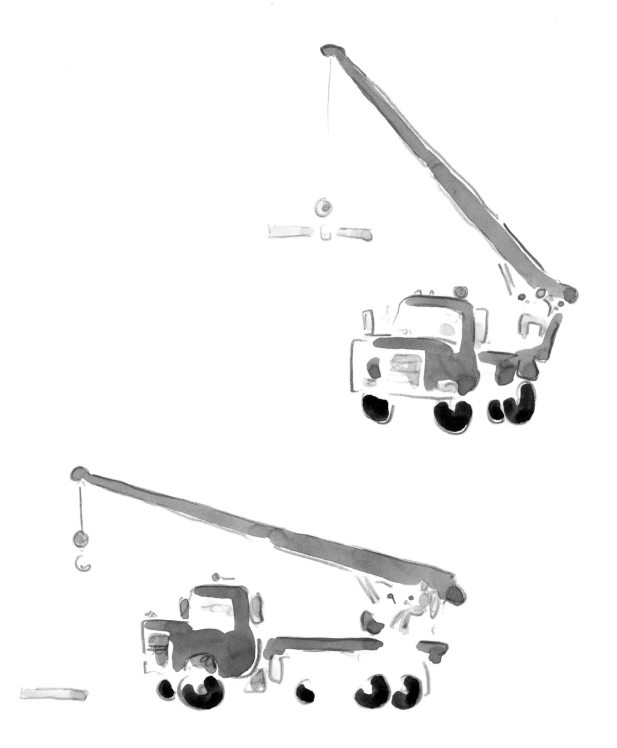

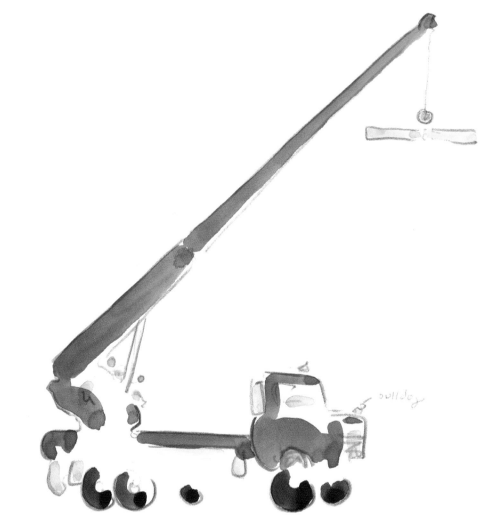

After a holiday weekend a crane arrives on the back
of a truck. It hooks wooden beams, hoists them into
the air, and sets them in place on top of the building.
The operator controls the crane with hydraulic levers
and the smallest movements of his fingers.

With the skeleton of the building in place, the skin goes on. A worker measures and marks plywood sheathing, leans into it with his knee, and nails it into place. Dark gaps in the wood make a changing face, with eyes and a mouth, then two mouths, then maybe it doesn't look like a face at all.

In early morning cold, workers huddle with their coffee. When the day gets warm, they take off their jackets. If it gets hot, some workers take off their shirts and their backs sweat. When it rains, workers cover the part of the building they are working on with plastic sheets, cover their heads with jackets, and trudge through mud to their trucks to stay dry. If it thunders and lightnings, everyone goes home.

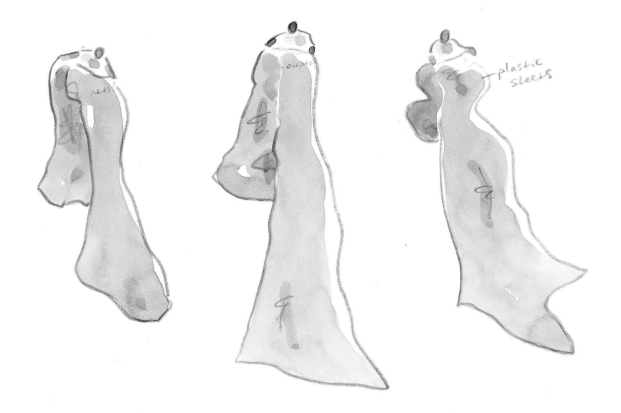

plastic
sleets

Fifty feet in the air a worker seals the roof's edges with a tool that looks like a gun but shoots caulk.

Other workers fit windows, nail siding, wedge insulation into walls, and start building floors

and the stairs between them. They rarely hit their toes, occasionally hit their thumbs.

Ladders stretch through the building,

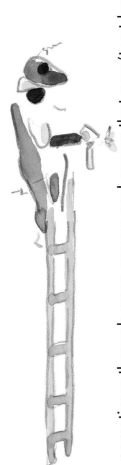

sometimes through open spaces and rooms that aren't yet built.

A worker welds together metal railings on the stairs.

The sparks are so hot they're white.

A contractor lugs toilets up stairs. She bumps into walls and can't see her feet.

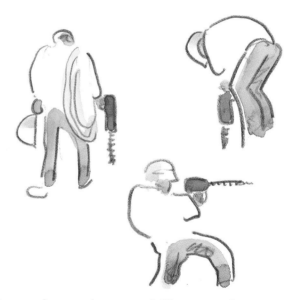

A worker takes a drill out of a metal briefcase and punches holes for electrical wires, smoke alarms, and phone jacks.

A worker tightens pipes to the toilets and sinks, then checks his work with a level.

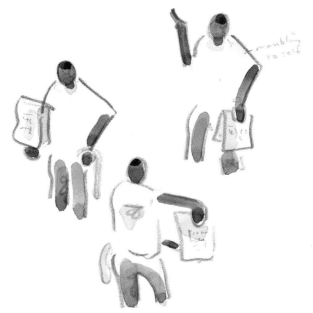

Another worker consults plans, shakes his head, then turns the plan right side up.

A radio plays and workers paint. Some days they hear the same song five times.

They prime wood and coat it, covering scratches, nicks and imperfections, pencil marks and jotted measurements—even one doodle of a moose.

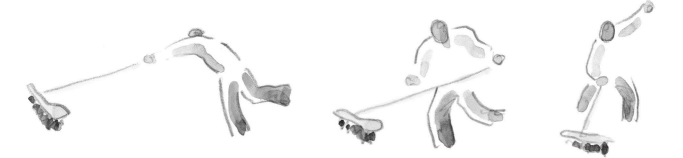

The building is just about finished. Workers sweep floors, pushing together piles of sawdust, crushed coffee cups, and the odd bent nail. Workers toss garbage through the open windows. Others dismantle scaffolding.

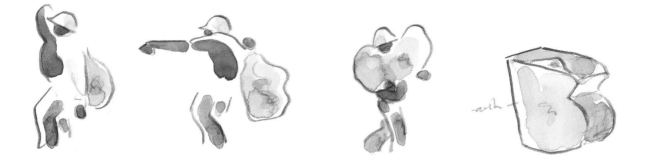

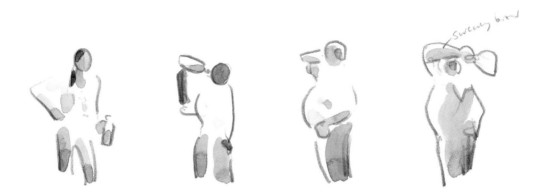

The architect brings iced tea and everyone gathers outside.
There's hand-shaking but not much talking. One worker
puts his hand on the side of the building and looks up.

This is a building. It stands between two other buildings not far from downtown. It stands empty, waiting to be filled with people. You can't hear the hammering, can't smell the concrete, can't taste the fried chicken, can't see the measured beams. But they are all part of the building, and you can feel them.

For my desk

Watercolors and pencil were used to prepare the full-color art.
The text type is Futura Medium.
Copyright © 1999 by Elisha Cooper
All rights reserved. No part of this book may be reproduced or utilized in any form
or by any means, electronic or mechanical, including photocopying, recording, or by
any information storage and retrieval system, without permission in writing
from the Publisher, Greenwillow Books, a division of William Morrow & Company, Inc.,
1350 Avenue of the Americas, New York, NY 10019.
www.williammorrow.com
Printed in Singapore by Tien Wah Press
First Edition 10 9 8 7 6 5 4 3 2 1

Library of Congress Cataloging-in-Publication Data
Cooper, Elisha.
Building / by Elisha Cooper.
p.   cm.
Summary: Describes the process of construction, step by step,
from clearing the site to cleaning up the finished building.
ISBN 0-688-16494-3
1. Building—Juvenile literature.
[1. Building.]   I. Title.   TH149.C66
1999   98-18902   CIP   AC